HOW TO BE JAMAICAN?

written by
Ken Maxwell
with illustrations by
Livingston McLaren

All complaints about this book should be
addressed, if possible in triplicate, and posted
to Livingston McLaren, Esquire, or Ken
Maxwell, Esquire, Jamaica Post Office. Perhaps it will reach them and perhaps they will
reply.

This book is dedicated to all those Jamaicans who have found that nowhere else in the world is real English spoken, and to those visitors who would like to take the opportunity to learn to speak properly.

PRINTING HISTORY

November 1981..........................First Printing
February 1987...........................Twenty-First Printing
October 1987............................Twenty-Second Printing
January 1988............................Twenty-Third Printing
May 1988................................Twenty-Fourth Printing
February 1989...........................Twenty-Fifth Printing
July 1989...............................Twenty-Sixth Printing
January 1990............................Twenty-Seventh Printing
May 1990................................Twenty-Eighth Printing
August 1990.............................Twenty-Ninth Printing
December 1990...........................Thirtieth Printing
March 1991..............................Thirty-First Printing
July 1991...............................Thirty-Second Printing
January 1992............................Thirty-Third Printing
June 1992...............................Thirty-Fourth Printing
September 1992..........................Thirty-Fifth Printing

ISBN 976–8001–21–6

Copyright © 1981 by Christopher Issa and Ken Maxwell.

Published by Jamrite Publications
14 Dominica Drive
Kingston 5
Jamaica.

§ Stephensons Litho Press Ltd.
9 Collins Green Avenue, Kingston 5.

A

A fe: "A fe me money". It is my money. "Fe" is used to indicate possession, as in "a fe him", "a fe dem" and so on. If anything is "a fe all", it belongs to everybody but no one maintains it.

A-go: "Me a-go now". I am going now, or "Me a-come". Also, an expression of intent, like "Me a-go kiss you". To which the correct reply is "Dat awrite".

Aise: "Him is too hard aise". He is too hard ears. He is unwilling to listen to advice or instructions.

1

Areddi: "Me ready areddi". I'm already prepared.

Anedda: "Give it anedda lick". Hit it again, in case you missed it the first time.

Are: "It's him are me". It is me or him.

A it mek: "A it mek you so ugly". That is why you are so ugly. That is the cause.

2

Arinj: Citrus fruit, known in overdeveloped countries as an orange.

Axe: "Don't axe me". Don't ask me, can be a simple statement, or, if used as an exclamation means, I know but I'm not telling you.

At: "What a pretty at you have on". A head covering. Also the opposite of cold. "What a way it at?"

Awrite: "Dat awrite". It's in order. I understand, I agree.

3

B

Badda: "No badda, it finish areddi". Don't bother, it is finished already. Can also mean worse, as "Him is badda dan me". He's worse than me.

Bare: "Is bare woman in de office". It does not mean that all the women in the office are naked, it means that there are only women in the office. Sorry about that. In other words, bare means only.

Bawl: "Bawl fe Tommy fe me". Call for Tommy for me. Also loud wails, usually at a funeral, especially if the deceased is known to you.

Baps: "Him get the job, and baps him lose it". Immediately, as in getting a cold. "As rain fall, baps she get a cold".

Bokkle: "Pass de rum bokkle". Pass the rum bottle.

Bredda: "You and me is bredda". You're my soul mate or occasionally, "We are brothers". Always affectionate and complimentary.

Bruk: "It bruk". The complete explanation for anything broken from a cup to a seized engine or a leg.

Bud: "See de bud there". There is the bird, always feathered. The other kind is a chick, or maybe a chile.

Bwaay: Total disbelief of the head scratching kind. "Bwaay! I thought he had sense".

Bwile: "Tea mek wid bwilin' water". Cold water is quite useless, contrary to restaurant practice.

Bwoy: Boy. Not necessarily a young male, a "bwoy" can be of any age, if he is your friend. "Come ya bwoy, mek me buy you a drink".

C

Cerfitikate: "Him get de marriage cerfitikate

from the parson". He (or she) got the marriage certificate from the clergyman. Not often used in Jamaica in this connection.

Chalklit: "Gimme a cup a chalklit, do". Please give me a cup of chocolate, usually made from local cocoa bought in the market, as what looks like a dark brown egg. Tinned cocoa is called "coco", so the difference is crucial.

Check: "Check me later". Talk to me later, let's meet later. If you say "I gwine check dat chick", it means, I'll look up that girl later.

Chewsday: "Me wi' see you on Chewsday, de day after Monday".

Chuck: "Cotch de chuck it full of feed". Put something under the wheel of the truck, it's full of feed.

Clawt: "What a pretty piece of clawt". Material usually for a suit or dress. When added to the end of a cuss word it intensifies it, as in "Rassclawt".

Coodeh: "Coodeh now, you see what happen". Look at that, you see what has happened. Can also mean look quickly, especially if repeated "Coodeh, Coodeh".

Cotch: "Beg you a cotch for the night". A short rest, either standing up or lying down. You can also "cotch a cyar" to prevent it running away on a hill.

Cris: Crisp. An expression of approval, usually a woman. "What a cris chile", sexy girl.

Cuyah: "Cuyah, see him there". Look at that, see him there. Can also convey surprise or incredibility as in "Cuyah!"

Cyan: "Me cyan go now, me busy". I can't go now, I'm busy.

Cyar: "Stop de cyar", if the brakes are good.

D

Dat: "Look pon dat now". Look at that now. Also, a word for pork, taken from a song "Give me some of dat".

Dawg: "Every dawg have 'im day". Every dog has his day. Everyone comes into their own eventually.

Dawta: "She is me dawta". She is my daughter or a woman you like.

De: "Where is de clawt". Where is the cloth. Also "di".

Dem: "De pickney dem". The children. Them is used to make plurals, as "de gal dem", "de cow dem", "de politician dem".

Depan: "Me depan haste" is to be in a hurry, whereas "me depan" means I'm busy doing something.

Dideh: "It dideh". There it is, see it there.

Dis: The opposite of "dat" of course.

Diyah: "Me diyah". I'm here, physically, or I've arrived.

Do: "Beg you a lift, do". Please give me a lift. If "do" is used to end a sentence, it always means please. If it starts a sentence, it indicates that a favour is about to be asked and that it is an important one, as in "Do, I beg you gimme a lift", so the lift is desperately needed.

Dun: "You dun yet?" Are you finished?

Dung: "Come dung out a de tree". Come down out of the tree. Also, of course, cows and horses make it. Smaller animals make a mess.

Duppy: "Me fraid a duppy, bwoy". I'm afraid of ghosts, boy. Duppies are found in grave-yards, cotton trees, and Rose Hall Great House.

Dutty: "What a dutty clawt". What a dirty cloth. To "drop in de dutty" is to fall to the ground.

Dweet: "Is me dweet". I did it. Not often used, usually it is likely to be "Is him dweet", or "Is dem dweet".

EEEE?: "EEEE? I cyan hear you". What? I can't hear you. A very quelling opening to a phone call.

Ef: "Ef you dweet, I will beat you". If you do it, I'll smack you.

Ello: How to answer the telephone, or you can try "EEEE?" instead.

F

Faass: "Him is too faass for me". Either too swift, or too impertinent for my liking, depending on context. When used of a girl, it is used as a compliment by men, and a criticism by women.

Facety: "What a facety bwoy". What a cheeky boy. When combined with faass, it covers all the undesirable qualities of a new generation.

Fambly: "We is fambly". We are related, of the same family.

Fiah: "It hot wid fiah". It is hot with fire, not with pepper.

Flim: "Have you any flim fe de camera?" You can also go to a flim, or watch an old flim on television.

Foot: "Him bruk 'im foot". Any part of the leg, from the sole of the foot as far as the thigh. "Foot bottom" is the sole.

Foreign: "Him come from foreign". Anywhere except Jamaica is foreign and everyone except Jamaicans are foreigners, as opposed to tourists, who are foreigners who have sensibly come to Jamaica for a visit.

Fram: "Me come fram Kingston". I live in Kingston, not simply that I have just arrived from Kingston.

Fren: "Him is me fren". He or she is my friend.

G

Galang: "Mek us galang now". Let us go along, opposite of "solong" which is a farewell.

Ganja: "You want some ganja?" Do you want some marijuana? Jamaica's most profitable crop, and more famous than rum. It is, however, still illegal here, in case you're interested.

Gellup: "Watch dat horse gellup". Watch that horse gallop. If we say "gellup-up" that intensifies the speed. If someone "Jes gellup up and dung" he is running around in ever decreasing circles, with its inevitable result.

Gimme: "Gimme a drink". Give me a drink. Usually to a friend. An order in a bar is usually, "Serve me a drink".

Ginnal: "Dat man a ginnal". That man is untrustworthy, unreliable, probably dishonest and not to be believed. To be called a ginnal is not really a compliment. A useful word.

Godeh: "Let we godeh now". Let's go there now. It can also, if used at the end of a sentence, mean Let's go.

Gordon: "What a pretty flowers gordon". A place for growing flowers. One may even have "a gordon kept by Mr. Garden" in which case it simply means that Mr. Gordon is in his garden. Very bewildering for foreigners.

18

Gravalishus: Greedy. "Me no like dat man, him is too gravalishus".

Gwine: "I gwine back home". That means, I'm going back to Jamaica, where else? "Gwine" means I'm going, either to a place, or to take a certain action. A declaration of intent.

H

Hab: "Him hab plenty money". He has plenty money. Can also mean have, had, or he possesses lots of money. Tenses mean little in Jamaican. We use them impartially and expect the listener to use their native wit to figure it out.

Hat: "It too hat fe hold". It is too hot to hold. It can also mean hurtful, as in "Me head a hat me" which means, I have a headache.

Heat: "Who heat my hegg?" Who has eaten my egg?

I

'Im: "See 'im dere". See him, her, she, he or it, there.

Ina: "Him ina worries". He is in worries usually financial, meaning trouble of some sort. Or, you can buy an ina tube for your car.

Irie: "It irie". It's okay, its first class, or that is excellent.

Isle: "I want some coconut isle". Coconut oil is used for frying and "kersine isle" is used for lamps, sometimes called kerosene oil.

J

Jah: "Praise Jah". Praise God. The old Bible name for Jehovah and most often used by Rastafarians.

RHAATID! ME INA A JAM...

Jam: "Him ina a jam". He is in a jam, usually over money. "Him jam the window". He has caused the window to stick either open or closed. "Him jam the car into gear". He forced the car into gear.

Jesum Piece: "You win a million dollars, Jesum Piece". Incredulity, or irritation.

Jancrow: "See a Jancrow there". There is a John Crow. A turkey buzzard, the unpaid scavenger of Jamaica, said to be named after a Rev. John Crow who leaned on his pulpit in a black gown, like a Jancrow drying his wings in the morning.

K

Kawn: "Buy some kawn for me". Buy some corn. Or you can "kawn" beef or pork using herbs, spices and pepper, and very good it is.

Kawz: "Is him kawz it". It is his fault, indeed it is always "him dat kawz it", for I can never kawz anything. It is always someone else.

Kibber: "Kibber de pat". Cover the pot please. When you are told to "kibber your mout", it means shutup and keep it shut. It is useful to know when to kibber you mout and always do this when in doubt.

Kiss: "Kiss me neck, my foot, me headside, me rass". All are expressions of surprise, incredulity, or defiance. If given unreasonable orders, by using one or another of these you can express refusal or surprise and whatever the results you can claim you meant something else.

Kyarri: "Kyarri it ya". Carry it here. Bring it here.

L

Laas: "It laas". It is lost, meaning simply I don't know where it is but I did not lose it. This is the explanation for anything that is missing. "Where is the tractor? It laas".

Lamps: "De man lamps me". The man fooled me, cheated me. Nothing to do with lights.

Lang: "Why you tek so lang" Why have you been so long? Or, "Don't lang out you tongue at me" meaning, don't stick out your tongue at me.

Lawd: "Lawd have mercy". Lord have mercy.

Lef: "De bus lef me". The bus left me, because I never miss a bus. It can also be the opposite of right, although on Jamaican roads it is best to be on "the right lef' han' side" meaning the correct left hand side of the road.

Liad: "Him is a liad". He is a liar, and somehow a liad is the worst kind of liar, probably congenital.

Lick: "I going give you a lick". You are not offering a taste, like a lollipop, but threatening to hit me. If I say "You lick hat" it means, it hurts physically.

Lickle: "Him is a lickle bwoy". He is a little boy, meaning small in stature. On the other hand, "lickle while" means, I'll be there soon.

M

Madda: "Where you madda is?" Where is mother?

Masa: "Listen, Masa, let me tell you". Once a term of respect, even subservience, meaning Master. Now used for emphasis or humour. "Big Masa", however, is still God.

Mashait: "Take the mashait and cut it". A machete or cutlass. The ubiquitous tool, peels oranges, sharpens pencils and cuts down trees.

Maskitta: "Why dem don't spray de maskitta dem?" Why don't they spray the mosquitos. Maskittas in Jamaica are no longer malarial but they still "bite hat", or sting painfully.

Mawga: "Look dat mawga dawg". Look at that meager dog, or that starving dog. Means slim when applied to people, emaciated when applied to animals.

Mek: "Mek me tell you". Let me tell you. "Mek hase" means hurry up, or make haste. You can also "mek de corner" or "mek up your mind".

Mout: "Shut you mout". Shut your mouth, or "kibber yu mout". If, however, you call your friend "a big-mout woman" it means she is a chatterbox, and doesn't know when to be silent.

N

Naa: "Me naa do it". I am not doing it. Total refusal.

Neegle: "Through the neegle's eye". The same that has been causing problems for the rich since Biblical times.

Nex: "Give me a nex drink". Give me another drink. You can also be "nex to a girl" or "have a nex friend".

Nutten: "Nutten ina dat". Nothing is in that, there is nothing to that.

Nyam: "You nyam too much". You eat too much.

O

Onda: "I onda the bed". Also a kind of Japanese car or motorcycle.

Ongle: "Is ongle me". It's only me. Of course, you can also have a sharp ongle in the road.

Ooman: "What a pretty ooman". What a pretty woman. "My ooman" may or may not be my wife, the terms are not necessarily the same.

Ooo: "Is ooo dat?" Who is that? If accompanied by "fe" it means whose is it, for instance, "Is ooo fe cyar?" means whose car is that?

Ouse: A dwelling, usually someone else's. My dwelling is "me yard".

Ove: "You ove any peas?" Do you have any peas?

Pickney: "Come here pickney". Come here child. The plural is "pickney dem".

Poas: "You poas me letter?" Did you post or mail my letter? A "poashole" is dug for a "fencepoas".

Priors: "The meeting began and ended with priors". The meeting began and ended with prayers.

Q

Quashie: "Is ongle quashie do dem tings". It is only the great unwashed, the lumpen, that do things like that. It can be either singular or plural, depending on the context, but never takes an "s".

R

Rada: "Me rada go to me bed". I prefer to go to my bed.

Rakstone: "It full a rakstone". It is full of rocks. A really big rock or boulder would probably be a "rass rakstone".

Rass: The single most important word in Jamaican speech. Originally meant backside, or ass, only more so. In addition it can now be an endearment, "You ole rass you". A term of abuse, "Him is a tiefing rass". Or, surprise and total amazement, "Rass!" It can also mean size, as in "A rass of a house".

Renk: "Don't be renk" Don't be impertinent, rude. Also, can mean that a person who is renk is difficult or evil smelling.

Rhaatid: "Don't get rhaatid". Don't get angry. If used as an exclamation expresses disbelief. "Rhaatid!"

Rydim: "All Jamaican music have rydim". All Jamaican music has rhythm. So have the women.

S

Satcherday: "Thank God tomorrow is Satcherday". Thank God tomorrow is Saturday.

Sinting: "What an ugly sinting" What an ugly something.

Soke: "Don't soke 'round me". Don't interfere with me. If on the other hand, you soke-up something, say a job, it means you've made a mess of it.

Sumody: "What a wonderful sumody". What a wonderful person.

Swimps: "Swimps and rice". A crustacean usually eaten fried with rice.

T

Tandey: "Tandey till me come". Stay there till I come.

Tankful: What you feel when you have given "tanks".

Tanks: Expression of gratitude, as in "Tanks very much", not a place for storing water. See "tenk".

Tart: "Me tart him gawn". I thought he'd gone. Past tense of think, not a prostitute.

Teet: "Him have bad teet". He has bad teeth. Not a mammary gland.

Tek: "Him tek de food". He took the food, that is to say, he stole it.

Tekeere: "Tekeere of the road" Take care of the road, beware of it, so take care when you're on it. Can also mean "Be careful" as in the farewell,"So long, tekeere".

Ting: "What a ting!" What a thing! However, if someone says "Mek us do a ting", if you are a woman watch how you answer. If you are a man, it simply means let's make an arrangement, to have a drink, do business, have a chat.

Tree: "Tree bwoy was in de tree". There were three boys in the tree. Depends on context whether it is a number or a plant.

Tun: "Tun 'back, you on de wrong road". Turn back, you've taken the wrong road. Also a weight.

Tups: "Give me a tups". Just give me a little.

U

Unnu: "Unnu is all idiot". You are all idiots.

Up: "Him mash up de car". He smashed the car only means it was a write-off. Everything is always more so if "up" is added, for instance "mash up", "bruk up", "feel up", "soke up".

V

Vencha: "Nothing vencha, nothing done".

W

Wa: "Say wa?" What did you say?

Wata: "Rum and wata please". Rum and water please.

Waters: "Him ina him waters". He is in his waters, he is drunk. "Waters" must not be confused with "wata", for "waters" always means hard drink, "wata" you bath in. To be "in your waters" does not mean you're in the swimming pool, though you can have "a waters in the wata". In other words, you can have a drink while you're having a swim.

Wid: "Him is wid she". He lives with her, they are living together. Strictly, it simply means with.

Wutless: "Some politician wutless". Some politicians are worthless.

Y

Yeye: "Me get something ina me yeye". I've got something in my eye. "Yeyewata" is tears.

Z

Zed: Last letter of the alphabet as "Fram A to Zed".

Ken Maxwell is a Jamaican farmer, broadcaster, journalist and clown. He was born in Vere, and has lived most of his life in Manchester and has a wife, a son and a daughter, three horses, two dogs, twenty cows and a twenty one year old car. He has spent his time looking ironically at life, and loves what he sees.

Livingston McLaren is an unsuccessful upholsterer, mechanic and motor repair man. His only success is in the field of cartooning, where he has won many prizes and awards for his honest and trenchant comments on local news. He has been awarded a Centenary Medal by the Institute of Jamaica, and a Musgrave Medal by the same institution, and his work has been exhibited since 1975 at the International Pavilion of Humour in Montreal.